T0028259

For Daniel, my moon. —IL

Special thanks to Marian L. Lewis, PhD, researcher and space
biologist employed by NASA (Johnson Space Center) during
the Apollo years, for her expert review of this text. Additional
thanks to award-winning children's author and science podcaster
Jennifer Swanson, for her wise and generous feedback.

MOON
SHOWER

Text copyright © 2023 by Irene Latham
Illustration copyright © 2023 by Myriam Wares

Published by Moonshower, an imprint of Bushel & Peck Books.
All rights reserved. No part of this publication may be reproduced
without written permission from the publisher.

Bushel & Peck Books is a family-run publishing house based in Fresno, California, that
believes in uplifting children with the highest standards of art, music, literature, and ideas.
Find beautiful books for gifted young minds at www.bushelandpeckbooks.com.

Our family is dedicated to fighting illiteracy all over the world. For every book we sell, we
donate one to a child in need—book for book. To nominate a school or an organization
to receive free books, please visit www.bushelandpeckbooks.com.

Type set in Tipique and LTC Kennerley.
Endpaper pattern licensed from Shutterstock.com

LCCN: 2023937752
ISBN: 978-1-63819-203-9

First Edition

Printed in Canada

1 3 5 7 9 10 8 6 4 2

THE
MUSEUM
ON THE
MOON

The Curious Objects on
the Lunar Surface

WRITTEN BY

IRENE LATHAM

ILLUSTRATED BY

MYRIAM WARES

CONTENTS

From 1961–72, NASA launched the first missions to the Moon, called the Apollo program. Six of those missions, Apollo 11, 12, 14, 15, 16, and 17, landed American astronauts on the lunar surface. The astronauts carried with them a variety of items that are now artifacts, including personal mementos, tools, equipment, memorials, and other things—like human waste products—that were unavoidable. The Moon truly is a museum!

WELCOME, EARTHLINGS!

Think you know the Moon
because you see it every night?
Imagine it's a museum, spend an afternoon—
then you'll know the Moon
is more than an empty, gray cocoon.
So many artifacts hide in plain sight!
Don't think you know the Moon
just because you see it every night.

On July 20, 1969, Apollo II astronaut Neil Armstrong stepped off the Lunar Module "Eagle" to become the first astronaut to leave something on the Moon—his footprints. Because the Moon has virtually no atmosphere, all human footprints remain on the Moon, just as they were, and will presumably be there for years to come.

FOREVER FOOTPRINTS

Human tracks tattoo
Moon's rutted face—

with no wind, no rain,
there's no way to erase

those cold, perfect
footprints

left to rest
forever in space.

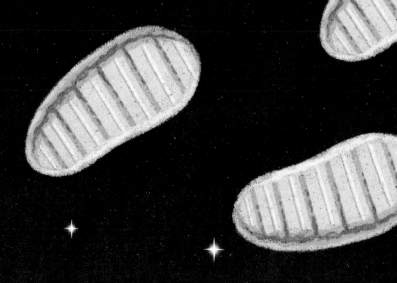

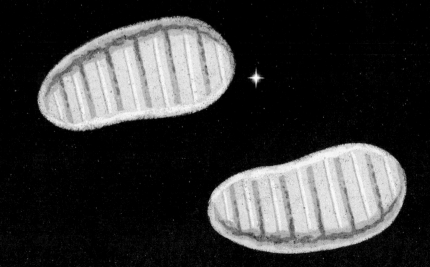

This flag is more
than just a bit of fabric

attached to a frame.
These stars ripple,

these stripes burst:
We were here!

Now time-tattered,
sun-battered

some fibers may be lost—
but pride roars.

Each of the six Apollo missions that landed on the Moon planted an American flag on the surface. Due to the lack of wind on the Moon, the astronauts mounted each nylon flag on a metal frame to make it *appear* to be flying.

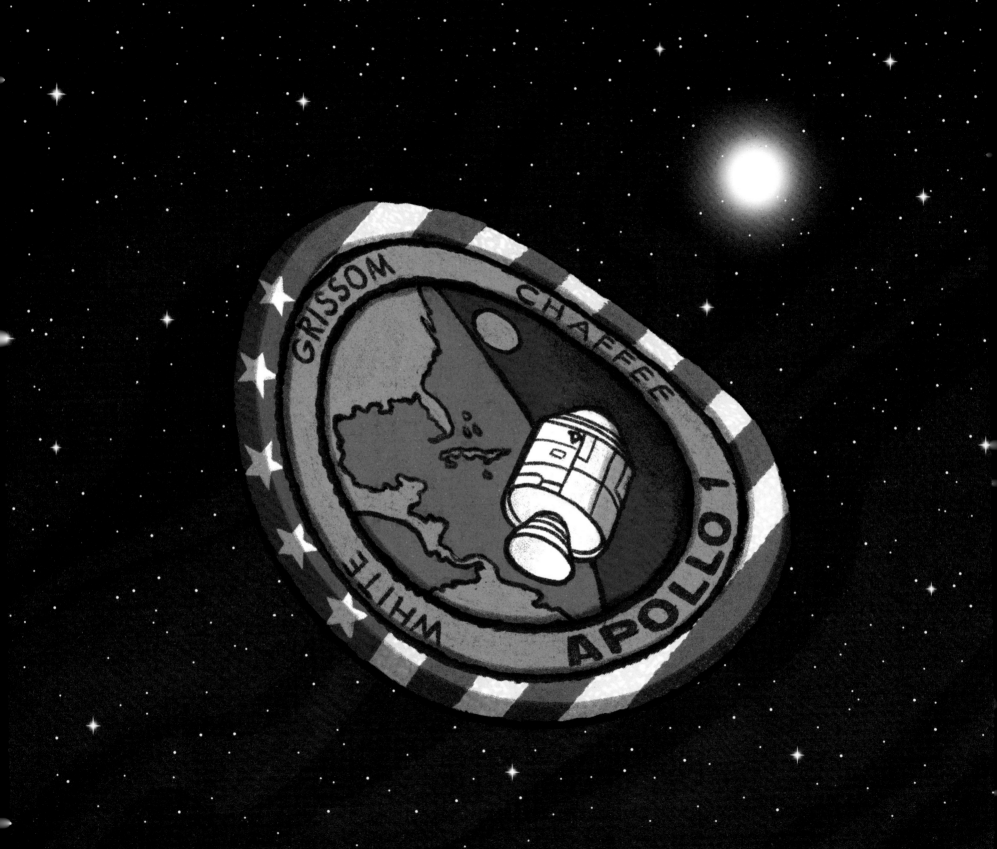

APOLLO I

A mission begins
and we learn

we make mistakes
and we learn

lives are lost
and we learn

we grieve
and we learn

we try again
and we learn

The first crewed mission of the Apollo program was set to launch in February 1967. A cabin fire during a launch rehearsal on January 27, 1967, claimed the lives of all three crew members—Gus Grissom, Ed White, and Roger Chaffee. The Apollo I patch recognizes the ultimate sacrifice made by those astronauts.

PHOTOGRAPH

One smiling family
makes its home
on the lunar floor—
astronaut-dad, mom,
and their two sons
make four!

Does this family enjoy
living on the Moon?
We sure hope so,
because they're not
coming back to Earth
anytime soon.

When Astronaut Charles
Duke visited the Moon as part
of the Apollo 16 mission in
April of 1972, he brought and
left his family's portrait. The
photograph includes himself
posing with his wife, Dorothy
Meade Claiborne, and their
sons, Charles Duke III (age 7)
and Thomas Duke (age 5).

In anticipation of success, the astronauts of the Apollo 11 mission brought with them an engraved plaque to leave on the Moon in commemoration of their historic achievement. The plaque rests at Tranquility Base, where they landed. It sits atop the Eagle's descent stage (the legs of the lunar module).

DEAR UNIVERSE,

Let me tell you about humans—We dream, discover, innovate. We came to the Moon to prove our daring in science and math. We found peace in the silence. We're not waiting for permission—next up, Mars! We all want more.

Sincerely,

Humankind.

PEACE

Peace is as
　　　an olive branch

Extended by astronauts
　　　from a wee blue planet

And left to glitter when kissed
　　　by the sun—a shiny

Crown of promises,
　　　a Moon-wish

Encrusted
　　　with science.

During the Apollo 11 mission, commander Neil A. Armstrong left a small (less than 6 inches in length) gold replica of an olive branch on the Moon's surface. The piece was meant to be a symbolic wish for peace for all humankind.

LITTLE FREE MOON LIBRARY

Just one book,
one sunburned book—

a Bible.
But that shouldn't be the only book.

Fat ones, thin ones;
fiction and nonfiction books.

Every reader knows
you can never have too many books!

People need friends,
and so do books.

If you come to the Moon,
please, please bring a book.

During the Apollo 15 mission, Commander Colonel David R. Scott left a Bible with a red cover perched on the dashboard of a lunar rover—which could be the start of a Little Free Library. The rover's remains are parked in the Moon's Sea of Showers in the Hadley Plains area of the Moon.

THEY GAVE MEDALS
TO THE MOON

two round bits of metal—
she holds them in her heart

a reminder of the great Space Race
and all who played a part

no room for words like "Cold War"
let your loyalties scatter

American or Soviet,
all contributors matter

two round bits of metal—
she holds them in her heart

Moon belongs to everyone
we can all play a part

The Space Race was basically a competition in the field of space exploration between nations—most prominently the United States and the Soviet Union. These same two countries were already enmeshed in a power struggle dubbed the "Cold War," which was related to the development of nuclear arms. Regardless of these differences, Apollo 11 astronauts wanted to recognize the contributions of two Soviet cosmonauts who perished in tragic accidents.

There are several "gardens of mirrors" on the Moon. Scientists call them lunar retroreflectors, or Lunar Laser Ranging RetroReflector array (LRRR). Laser pulses sent from Earth bounce off the mirrors and return to Earth, providing precise measurements (to the centimeter!) of the Earth-Moon distance. The average distance between the Earth and the Moon is 238,855 miles (384,400 km), depending upon their position.

HOW TO DETERMINE THE DISTANCE BETWEEN US AND THE MOON

plant a   garden
of mirrors

                snug in Moon soil

water it
with laser   beams,

time   and patience.

watch calculations

            grow

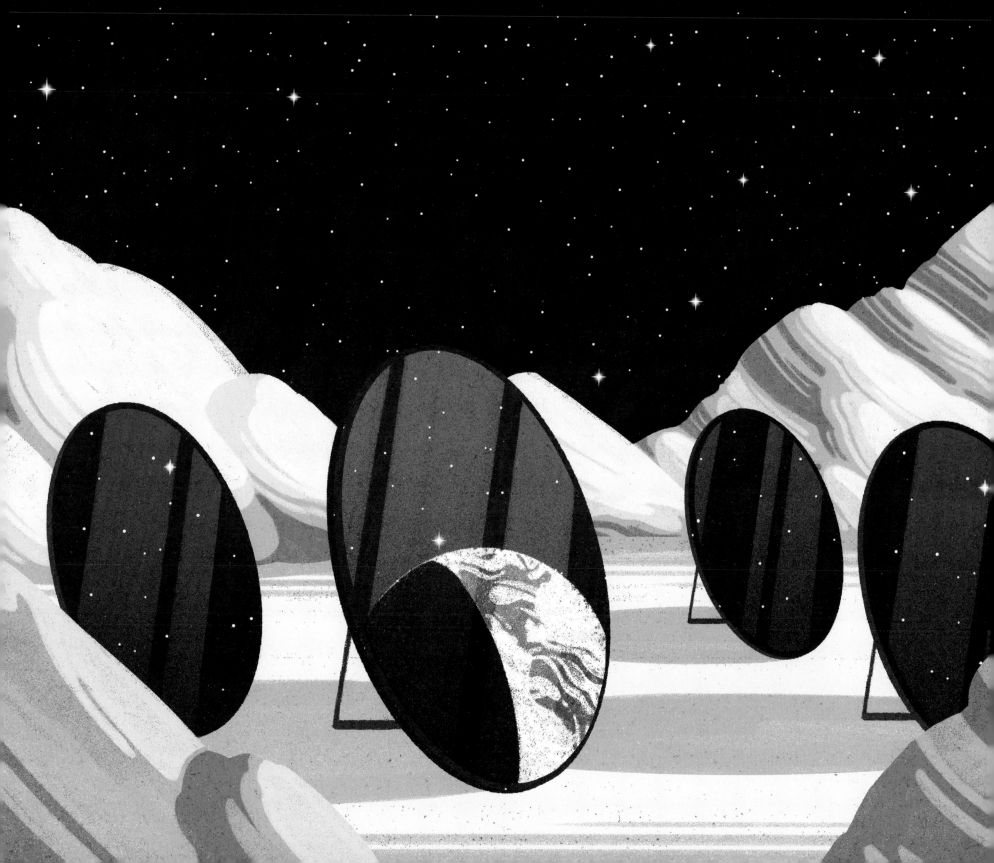

Bring your own golf balls.
En route to the Moon

fashion a club by attaching
a smuggled-aboard clubhead

to the arm
of a sample collection device.

Remember: your spacesuit
will be bulky, inflexible.

Don't expect your game to be
the same as it is on Earth.

Every shot is a bunker shot
on the Moon.

But, oh, when ball connects—
listen to the stars cheer!

During the Apollo 14 mission in 1971, Astronaut Alan Shepard hit two golf shots using a modified club he made himself. The two balls went 24 yards and 40 yards, respectively, and remain lodged in moondust.

During the Apollo 15 moonwalk, Commander Colonel David R. Scott performed a live demonstration of Galileo's theory for TV cameras. The hammer and the falcon feather used in the experiment still rest on the Moon.

GRAVITY

Galileo said—

whether heavy

                              or light

              whatever is released together
              falls together

and now we know it's true
because it was on TV for all to see:

a falcon feather

                              a hammer

              falling
              falling

hitting Moon's crust
at exactly the same time.

                              Rewind!

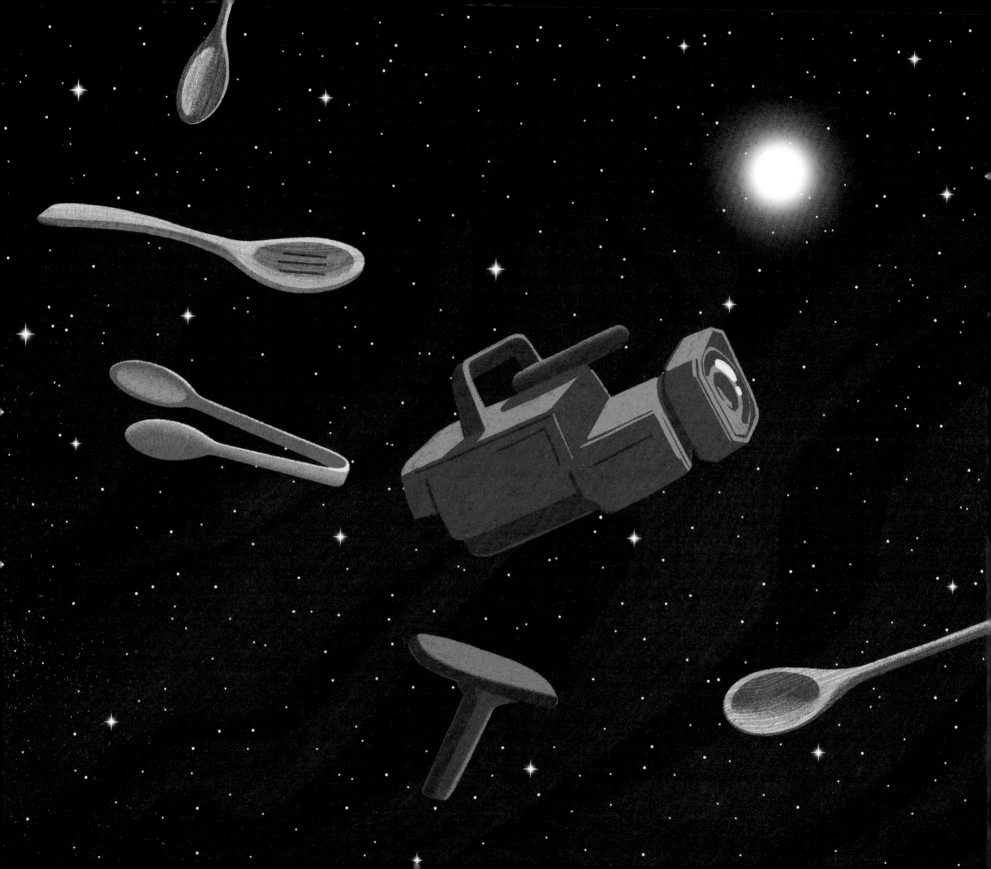

TOSS ZONE

Just eight minutes to shed
any ounces of excess—
Goodbye, scoops and tongs,
so long, uncomfortable armrests!

That tube that carried the flag?
Buh-bye!
That heavy TV camera?
Better to let it stay in the sky.

Oh, Moon. We're so sorry.
We did what we had to do.
But we never meant to make
a dump out of you.

When time came for Apollo
II astronauts to return to the
ship, Mission Control was
concerned about the safety
of their return voyage.
After all, they now had 48
additional pounds of Moon
rock and soil samples. To
account for the weight
difference, the astronauts
had to toss whatever
they could to ensure the
spacecraft had enough
power to carry its contents
and the crew back to Earth.

MOON'S MESSAGE UPON READING THE APOLLO 11 SILICON DISC

Apollo 11 astronauts left on the Moon a small silicon disc, not much larger than a half-dollar coin. It contains messages from U.S. Presidents and 73 other countries and features intricate artwork and words with letters so tiny they can only be read with a microscope.

Me, Moon.
Brilliant. Tranquil. Good.

A home beyond time.
Earth's nearest neighbor

and on this occasion,
the road to man's oldest dream.

      Sky
      light.

Clear mirror of peace
bringing together

stars
and courage.

Unshakable. Wild. Beautiful.
Me, Moon.

MEET THE MAGNIFICENT MOON DUO

Ebb & Flow
come and go
mapping
spinning
finding gravity
fields on the Moon

Ebb & Flow
whine and slow
grinding
dying
crashing
twins together
on the Moon

About the size of a home washer and dryer, Ebb & Flow were the names given to the twin spacecraft that were launched September 10, 2011, as part of the GRAIL (Gravity Recovery and Interior Laboratory) mission that used high-quality gravitational field mapping to determine the Moon's internal structure.

Have you ever wondered how astronauts go to the bathroom in space? Since space suits can't be taken off, you've got a mess waiting to happen! Astronauts during the Apollo missions wore collection bags inside their suits—a not-always-reliable method. Several of these collection bags currently dot the Moon's surface.

ASTRO NOT

astro arm
astro knee
astro poop
astro pee

astro what?
astro yes
can't hold it!
astro mess!

astro nut
astro not
only human—
astronaut

THE JUNK SIDE OF THE MOON

What's an astronaut to do
when there's no place to dump space junk?
No compactor or incinerator;
no dumpster or landfill.

When there's no place to dump space junk,
old lunar probes and orbiters pile up.
The Moon itself becomes a junkyard
for waste that weighs too much to send home.

Hello, pile of old lunar probes and orbiters!
It's time to figure out what to do with you.
Space junk that weighs too much to send home
needs consideration, too.

Yes, it's time to solve this problem—
before we junk up the Moon.
With no compactor or incinerator,
what's an astronaut to do?

Space junk on the Moon largely consists of equipment. More than 70 spacecraft vehicles had to be left behind due to weight and cost concerns. If humans were able to develop the technology to safely reach and return from the Moon, surely we can invent a solution to the Moon's trash problem, too.

The ashes of Eugene M. Shoemaker were launched in a tiny (1 3/4 inches long and 7/10 inches in diameter) polycarbonate memorial capsule aboard Lunar Prospector to the Moon. A distinguished astrogeologist with the U.S. Geological Survey, he was killed July 18, 1997, in a car crash without ever achieving his dream of going to the Moon.

EPITAPH

Here lies Gene,
gone too soon.

He always
wanted to go
to the Moon.

Our bodies
may crumble,
words may rust—
but dreams
are made
of moondust.

Here lies Gene,
gone too soon.

Forever now
at home
on the Moon.

Some of the most important
things left on the Moon you
can't see with human eyes.
Astronauts brought our culture
to the Moon, our knowledge,
and so much hope! Each time
we look to the Moon, it glows
with possibility, awakening new
mysteries and proving what
humans can do when we set a
goal in motion.

INVISIBLE

If stardust is made of human
hopes and prayers,
every wish·upon·a·star—

then moondust
is layer upon layer
of our dreams·come·true—

the glow that ignites
maybe too

me   and   you.

THIS POEM IS AN OUTPOST ·

More than just a museum—

imagine a research hub,
a living lab,

a luminous home
away from home.

Get ready—you could
be the one

to wheel a lunar rover
over craggy hills and seas.

You can join others from
across the globe

to preserve Moon's legacy
and make yet another

giant   leap—

The new dream for the
museum on the Moon is
that it should be expanded
to include a base camp
somewhere near the Moon's
south pole. There, scientists
from across the globe will
be able to live together,
experiment, and innovate—
in hopes of developing
ways for human life to
thrive on other worlds.

MORE ABOUT OUR MOON'S MUSEUM

HUMANS WHO WALKED ON THE SURFACE OF THE MOON (SO FAR)

Apollo 11 (July 16–24, 1969)
Neil Armstrong (Aug. 5, 1930–Aug. 25, 2012)
Edwin "Buzz" Aldrin (Jan. 20, 1930–)

Apollo 12 (November 14–24, 1969)
Charles "Pete" Conrad Jr. (June 2, 1930–July 8, 1999)
Alan Bean (Mar. 15, 1932–May 26, 2018)

Apollo 14 (January 31–February 9, 1971)
Alan B. Shepard Jr. (Nov. 18, 1923–July 21, 1998)
Edgar D. Mitchell (Sept. 17, 1930–Feb. 4, 2016)

Apollo 15 (July 26–August 7, 1971)
David R. Scott (June 6, 1932–)
James B. Irwin (Mar. 17, 1930–Aug. 8, 1991)

Apollo 16 (April 16–27, 1972)
John W. Young (Sept. 24, 1930–Jan. 5, 2018)
Charles M. Duke Jr. (Oct. 3, 1935–)

Apollo 17 (December 7–19, 1972)
Eugene Cernan (Mar. 14, 1934–Jan. 16, 2017)
Harrison H. Schmitt (July 3, 1935–)

For a complete listing of the Apollo missions, please visit: https://www.britannica.com/story/timeline-of-the-apollo-space-missions.

MOON MILESTONES

September 13, 1959: First spacecraft to land on the Moon (and first human artifact in the "museum," located near the Sea of Serenity)—Luna 2 (U.S.S.R.)

October 7, 1959: First picture of the far side of the Moon—Luna 3 (U.S.S.R.)

February 3, 1966: First spacecraft to soft land on the Moon—Luna 9 (U.S.S.R.)

December 24, 1968: First humans to orbit the Moon—Apollo 8: Frank Borman, James Lovell, William Anders (U.S.)

July 1969: First space cooperation between nations—U.S. And U.S.S.R. (Soviets released flight plans for Luna 15 to ensure it did not collide with Apollo 11)

July 20, 1969: First human to walk on the Moon—Apollo 11: Neil Armstrong (U.S.)

September 24, 1970: First return of lunar samples by an unmanned spacecraft—Luna 16 (U.S.S.R.)

January 3, 2019: First robotic landing on the Moon's far side—Chang'e 4 (China)

ADDITIONAL NOTES

"Welcome, Earthlings!"

This poem is a triolet: a poem with eight lines in which line one repeats in lines four and seven and line two repeats in line eight to create the following rhyme scheme: abaaabab. The primary goal of the United States' NASA Apollo program (1961–1972) was not to create a museum. The program aimed to establish space technology, carry out scientific exploration of the Moon, and to develop ways for humans to work in the lunar environment. For a complete list of all the curious objects left on the Moon, please visit: NASA's Catalog of Manmade Material on the Moon https://history.nasa.gov/FINAL%20Catalogue%20of%20 Manmade%20Material%20on%20the%20Moon.pdf

"Forever Footprints"

View footage of Neil Armstrong's first step here: https:// www.cbsnews.com/video/watch-neil-armstrongs-first- steps-on-the-moon/

"Old Glory"

Of the six flags planted on the Moon, it's thought that the flag from Apollo 11 was destroyed by exhaust during the lunar module's liftoff. High resolution images captured by the Lunar Reconnaissance Orbiter show the other five flags are still standing, but we won't know their condition until we return to the Moon.

"Apollo I"

It was the Apollo 11 crew who placed the Apollo 1 patch on the Moon. It's important to note that all Apollo missions–not just the "successful" ones or the crewed ones—resulted in learning and were essential in achieving the goals of the U.S. Space program.

"Photograph"

Charles Duke, who brought along the photo of his family, served as the mission's lunar module pilot. Along with crew commander John Young, he spent an amazing 71 hours on the Moon's surface.

"Dear Universe,"

This poem is written as a Golden Shovel poem: a poem inspired by a line of poetry, text, or quote (called a "striking" line). The ending word of each line of the poem, when read top to bottom, composes that striking line. The plaque left on the Moon provides the striking line for this Golden Shovel: "We came in peace for all mankind."

"Peace"

This poem is written as an acrostic: the first letter of each line (or in this case, the first letter of each stanza) creates a word or phrase.

"Little Free Moon Library"

This poem is a ghazal: an Arabic poetry form that employs couplets and repetition, most often to tackle topics of love and loss. The once-red cover of the Bible on the Moon has likely faded to white, due to the intensity of the sun's rays. Little Free Libraries are neighborhood book exchanges operated by people just like you. Currently more than 150,000 Little Free Libraries are registered and operating around the world. Why not have one on the Moon, too? Learn more at littlefreelibrary.org.

"They Gave Medals to the Moon"

The Apollo 11 crew left two medals on the Moon. One medal was for space pioneer Yuri Gagarin, the first human to orbit the Earth, who died aboard a routine training flight accident in a jet plane March 1967. The other medal was for Vladimir Komarov, who was killed just a month later at the end of his Soyuz 1 solo test flight when his spacecraft's descent parachute failed to open.

"How to Determine the Distance Between Us and the Moon"

In addition to information about distance, lunar retroreflectors also help to map the lunar surface and provide clues about the Moon's (liquid) core. It's because of the presence of this simple tool that we now know the Moon spirals approximately 3.8 cm further away from Earth each year. Find out more about the distance between the Earth and the Moon, including how long it takes to get to the Moon at https://www.rmg.co.uk/stories/topics/how-far-away-moon.

"Alan Shepard's Advice for Golfing on the Moon"

Alan Shepard reportedly practiced his golf shot while in quarantine before the mission, and it's during that time that he discovered the space suit's bulkiness would only allow him to hit the shot one-handed.

"Gravity"

Experiments on the Moon require much advance thought and planning. Because their lunar module was named "Falcon," a falcon feather (along with a second backup falcon feather) was collected prior to the mission to be used to demonstrate Galileo's theory of gravity.

"Toss Zone"

Archaeologists use the term "toss zone" in their site work and study of artifacts left behind by ancient civilizations. What remains in a toss zone is valuable for what it reveals about what a community deems important, and what it considers expendable.

"Moon's Message Upon Reading the Apollo II Silicon Disc"

This is a "found" poem: a poem created by selecting words from an existing text. In this case, the text was the Apollo 11 Silicon Disc, as published in *We Came in Peace for All Mankind: The Untold Story of the Apollo 11 Silicon Disc* by Tahir Rahman (Leathers Publishing, 2008). The poem contains words found in the messages from the following countries: Afghanistan, Australia, Brazil, Canada, Chile, Costa Rica, Greece, India, Iran, Italy, Ivory Coast, Kenya, Korea, Latvia, Mali, Philippines, South Africa, Vietnam, and Zambia. It's important to note that silicon technology was developed specifically for this mission, with only a three-week turnaround time. Today silicon is used in the construction of nearly everything we own.

"Meet the Magnificent Moon Duo"

The names "Ebb" and "Flow" were given to the probes after a national contest won by 4th grade students at Emily Dickinson Elementary School in Bozeman, Montana. Once the pair of probes began to weaken and age, they were purposefully crashed into a mountain at the Moon's north pole on December 17, 2012. The crash site was named for Sally Ride, the first American woman astronaut in space.

"Astro Not"

While it's unfortunate that astronauts had to leave behind these human waste collection bags, scientists are excited to learn what these samples may reveal about the effects on humans of long-term exposure to Moon conditions. Current-day astronauts no longer use unreliable collection bags. They use Maximum Absorbency Garments, a fancy name for adult diapers.

"The Junk Side of the Moon"

This poem is a variation of a pantoum: a series of quatrains, with the second and fourth lines of each quatrain repeated as the first and third lines of the next; the last line of the poem is the same as the first line of the poem. The Apollo scientists and engineers were focused on achieving the goals of their missions, not on keeping the Moon clean. Other crewless missions, including those from Europe, Japan, Russia, and the United States, have also contributed to the problem.

"Epitaph"

Eugene M. Shoemaker was best known for his work on extraterrestrial impacts and for his later collaboration with his wife, Carolyn, in the study and discovery of comets. An *epitaph* is a brief few words that are written, spoken, or inscribed on a tombstone in memory of someone who has died.

"Invisible"

Humans are drawn to the Moon and its mysteries. And, wherever one lives on the Earth, we all share the same Moon. Perhaps it's the invisible things the Moon represents that inspire poets and artists to create "Moon" pieces.

"This Poem Is an Outpost"

Humans haven't set foot on the Moon in more than a half century, but NASA's Artemis program aims to change that. If the schedule holds, new astronauts will plant their boots in lunar soil as early as 2025. Private companies like SpaceX and Blue Origin are also designing their own lunar exploration programs.

ABOUT THE CREATORS

Irene Latham, Author

Irene Latham is the author of many books for children, including novels, poetry, and picture books. Winner of the 2016 ILA Lee Bennett Hopkins Promising Poet Award, she writes poetry inspired by nature, art, and the experience of being human. Together with Charles Waters, she's written *Dictionary for a Better World* and *Can I Touch Your Hair? Poems of Race, Mistakes and Friendship*, which was named a Charlotte Huck Honor book and a Kirkus Best Book of 2018. Irene lives on a lake in Alabama, where she and her husband have been known to take the boat out at night for dreamy moongazing sessions.

Myriam Wares, Illustrator

Myriam Wares is a French-Canadian illustrator from Montreal. Her work touches on a variety of themes, notably natural sciences and technology, mythology and surrealism, as well as contemporary social issues. With a rich but subtle layering of textures and the dramatic use of lighting, she creates warm, surrealistic scenes that draw viewers into a world of wonder. Initially a self-taught artist, she later completed her professional training in illustration at Dawson College. She has worked with clients from around the world on projects ranging from packaging design to editorial illustration, publishing, and advertising. Her work has been recognized and awarded by organizations such as Communication Arts, World Illustration Awards, and *3x3 Magazine*.